# Skating
## Among the Graves

BOOKS BY GERALDINE RUBIA

A Poem In My Soup        1980

*Contributing co-editor*

Newfoundland Writers  1974
From This Place          1977
A Way With Words      1987

# Skating
## Among the Graves

### Geraldine Rubia

killick press
an imprint of Creative Publishers

St. John's, Newfoundland
1991

© 1991, Geraldine Rubia

The publisher acknowledges the financial contribution of the *Cultural Affairs Division of the Department of Municipal and Provincial Affairs, Government of Newfoundland and Labrador*, which has helped make this publication possible.

Appreciation is expressed to the *Canada Council* for publication assistance.

Cover Drawing by Janice Udell
Courtesy of Christina Parker Gallery
from the collection of Ilse Hughes

Printed in Canada by:
ROBINSON-BLACKMORE PRINTING & PUBLISHING LTD.
P.O. Box 8660, St. John's, Newfoundland A1B 3T7

Published by:
KILLICK PRESS (AN IMPRINT OF CREATIVE PUBLISHERS)
*A Division of Robinson-Blackmore Printing & Publishing Ltd.*
P.O. Box 8660, St. John's, Newfoundland A1B 3T7

Canadian Cataloguing in Publication Data

Rubia, Geraldine.

    Skating among the graves

    Poems.
    ISBN 0-920021-97-2

I. Title.

PS8585.U24S52  1991      C811.'54      C91-097577-9
PR9199.3.R82S52   1991

*This book is dedicated to*
*Bernice Morgan, Helen Porter*
*and Berkley Reynolds*

*There are some things so serious you have to laugh at them.*

Niels Bohr (1885–1962), Danish physicist

# Table of Contents

## *All Stark and Lonely Things*

What can you see in that, they ask when I exclaim
at sight of twisted driftwood on a beach,
a dispossessed, contorted limb
the sea has bleached bone white,
or when I stop to view the winter tree
that stands against the sky making lace,
or find myself at the face of a barren cliff entranced.

What do you see in him, they'd ask me if they knew
I love this awkward, inarticulate man,
who feels in honour bound
to scorn all grace and tenderness,
who rarely lets a lover's smile break through,
but stands against the world in his place
and never speaks his love but denies it forcibly.

I revel in the tender word and glance,
the summer tree, the rose, the rampant grass,
all lovely things before they fade and pass give pleasure—
but the stubborn man, the rock, the naked tree
touch something deep and still;
all stark and lonely things sing out to me.

### Places That Were

These were outports
when we came this way before
but now are merely
landmarks on the shoreline:
Richard's Harbour
Cape la Hune
Dog Cove
Cul de Sac.
It seems as if the boat
must slacken speed
but no, we go on by,
the Captain trying to make us see
(academic question now)
the only point
at which a boat
could safely venture in.

Yet there are places
still for us to go
where children run to wharf or hill
to wave a welcoming:
Grand Bruit, Piccaire,
La Poile, Rencontre West,
Francois, McCallum; but in all
we know that now
already is past tense
nostalgic history
a fast receding backdrop
for newer ways of life
in road-connected towns,
the chance to work
or fight
or plead for better days.

Here, we will say,
were things that really mattered:
the stubbornness of fishermen
who built another boat
as soon as one was battered
on the rocks;
the faith of women
coaxing scanty soil
to nourish rhubarb roots
and bleeding hearts
and flowers whose names
they never knew;
the still childlike children
climbing barefaced cliffs
and painting stars
to prove that they'd been there.

Here a thunderous waterfall
forever drowned
the sound of the sea
and the moaning wind
that tried to wrench
the cabled church from the rock
while black sheep
calmly chewed;
here you could see the sun set twice
if you walked away
from the shade of a hill
to where the light was golden
still striking into henhouse doors
along the yard-wide road;
cemeteries, of course,
but one you could not see
behind a hill where there was earth
enough to bury the dead;
and another carpeted
from end to end
with wild blue irises.

All, we will say,
seemed either right or human:
one man thought it hard
to go and seek the Dole
when his summer's catch was small;
another never did a tap
and thought that all
the government might give
was scarcely half his due;
no neighbour went unhelped
whose luck turned bad
and the child who said
"I got no father, sir"
seemed not to carry
mortifying scars.

Though no way out is seen
from certain sheltered coves,
the way is there
between the lines of land
and over it will pass
the last livyers
on the last boat
abandoning wharves
to the unchecked waves;
the good luck mat
will fade on the back porch floor,
wicks dry out
in rejected lamps
and holy pictures blankly gaze
from the walls of empty rooms.

I wonder
will anyone try
to find the passage back.

A narrow path
a rock on a mossy bluff
some juniper, fern, and goldenrod

a quiet pond —
this might be enough
if I had never known the ocean

### One at a Time

I do not feel affection
for the Portuguese en masse
gale-warned fishermen clog-shoeing Water Street
four-a-breasting sidewalks so you cannot pass
oozing unadulterated odors of the fleet

But sometimes in the evening
I have seen one passing by
hands a-pocket, slowly ambling on
fishing-seasoned exile with no homing sigh
but whisper-whistled snatches of an orphaned song

## *Threshold*

I have been a long time
travelling to this place
mistaking no other for it
on the way

Here is
my lasting habitation
a warm room
or northern waters

I dare not imagine
whiffs of smoke
and licks of flame
from a banked fire

More likely
reflected sunlight
from the iceberg's tip

## *My House*

My house is freezing
how can I leave my house
to shiver into pieces

My house is drowning
how can I leave my house
to be swept away in the flood

My house is burning
how can I leave my house
to shrivel into ashes

## Leave-Taking

Rock-forbidden roses on her walls
gleaming kettle coming to a boil
no neighbours any more for tea
who needed them
her home was all.
Thin driftwood brittle fingers
clutching at her door
she faces her husband
on the rain-bright pebble path

       "I'm not going, I tell you.
       What's there for me?"
       (Old devil, he
       always was the one
       to gad about)

Bone-forbidden sea behind his back
no nets to mend
no boat to haul up on the rocks
another dwelling waiting for his touch
paint peeling fence falling
naked for a porch,
neighbours there
to yarn with on the wharf.
He pries the clinging fingers loose

       "Come on now mother,
       you'll love it, wait and see."
       (Stubborn old woman, she
       always was the one
       to make a fuss)

## *Forecast*

A small boy in a wild cove
tells off the swaggering sea;
toes gripping wet pebbles
he shouts into the uproar
"shut your big mouth you,
go on, go out!"
and sees the blustering bully
back up at his command.

It takes a little time
of traipsing on the barrens
exposed
to the whole mocking almanac
until the boy slips quietly
into a self-scooped pool
and vanishes at last
like
jettisoned
treasure.

## *Looking for a New Anthem*
### *(Newfoundland)*

Crawling, running, pushed, pulled
into the True North's second century
extolling, bemoaning, ignoring
four and more of our own
singing all the anthems
wanting only one
or none.

Wallowing in Prattian tides
tracing our features on a cliff
swearing and denying
that the wise and rugged livyer
really did exist,
we trick Her Majesty's Government
to hand out generously
and we cry abuse! abuse!
what now the smiling land.

Hold fast to the older easygoing ways!
Give us everything that's new!
We apologize and take offence
justify, criticize
shame, shame on the baby-swallowing ditches
what will the market bear
in high-riser rents
long to reign over us
dollars and cents.

An anthem to an ancient child
confused, immobilized?
No.

Sing to a spawning caplin
pressed on either side
between old myths
and new insanities.

### The Astronomer Says It's Impossible for the Poet/Naturalist to Whistle Six Consecutive Notes From le Sacre du Printemps

(After Harold Horwood and Dora Russell
in *The Evening Telegram*, 1965)

our
springtime's cummings in
glad awe of carpenter* in
green-blooded rivulets
beneath the great (t)horned (c)owl of
Goat Cove Canyon
whistles and whisks
the sacred dust
off a dormant ladybug
who
does not feel
what time it is
caught in the shimmering currant
of

*wood louse

### In Bowring Park

May morning pool ...
   cool uncluttered ducks
      easing over oiled silk
       ...

The fierce gull
   has plucked a dandelion flower ...
      oh no! the yellow duckling
       ...

So-white coconut flakes
   on this cinnamon bush ...
      chuckley-pear blossoms

### Has There Ever Been

I was born catching my breath
at reflections, shapes, and shades
but in the half-century since
has there ever been
so windowful a moon
such luminous clusters of moon coins
so glowing a gold-vermilion sun
pulsing suns around suns

Has there ever been
since that high holy mountain
a face with so blazing a light
melting wide entryways
to this guarded dwelling
coaxing improbable fruit
from this predictable tree

One of these held-breath days
when the sun is drawing water
I will exhale myself
up a silvery shaft
and infuse its fervent circumference
freely caressing your eyes
until back of the black thin edge of time
we are at last the light

The sun, too,
is n o n - c o m m i t t a l ;
shows no provable signs
of basking in our worship
or blushing at our shameless
a v i d i t y  f o r  h i s  p r e s e n c e – a
presence denied us only by ord-
inate interventions or self-
banishment to sterner climates;
he is always where he is
supposed to be and
a l w a y s   s h i n i n g
shining.

### *Skating on Thick Ice*

The frozen lake is long and wide
and brilliantly incites
the gash and glide of restless blades,
but here around the solid edge
where faded rushes show above the ice,
the cautious skater
shades his eyes
and stalks the glinting day.

Ignoring headlong fools
who etch the length and breadth
with iridescent doodling,
he moves inside his narrow arc
with calculated ease,
achieves a sort of virtuosity
but risks no scraped and bloody shins
from dashing past his mark.

He keeps his poise,
embellishing mistakes,
receives some mild applause
from those who do not skate at all,
and if the lake unseasonably
should crack beneath his feet,
there are no depths where he can fall —
he will simply stop
in his splintered tracks.

## Snow

In the snowflake on my sleeve
I can with naked eye perceive the feathery precision,
and a magnifying glass would show
a bioplastic vision of unique geometry
which in the aggregate
confounds all transportation
cancels life
and houses Eskimo.

How sad to see the exquisite filigree
dissolve into the moss of my all-weather coat,
how shattering to note the brown and splattery mush
of a downtrodden multitude
which would in lonelier places
upstage starlight.

Just now I rue the melting
of each ethereal doily
and would keep the master handiwork intact,
but in fact if some celestial aide
should dial eternal frost
then lost and bedazzled in my crystal mausoleum
I would expire screaming
for a patch of gaudy grass.

I am walking with you tirelessly
through wide summer meadows, climbing
easily the fences in between;
among tall trees on scarcely pathways,
feet springing on the green-
shadowed moss; bending to pick
cool orange crackerberries
I trip on a trailing root or bough
and reach for you to steady myself:

> striding laughing towards the now-
> shining at the edge of the grove
> do you feel my arm linked in yours?

I am skating with you effortlessly
down the long pond, avoiding
gracefully hazards of crusted snow;
through night spangle on a moon pathway,
blades ringing, swift into slow-
measured movement; looking to catch
a silent fire-cracker star
I stumble on a crystal ledge
and reach for you to save myself:

> gliding laughing to the edge
> of the shining dark imprisoned pool
> do you feel my hand clasped in yours?

I am flying with you fearlessly
through the endless air, confiding
skilfully in currents cross and kind;
breasting headwinds in the pathless heavens,
all singing in the blind-
lifting sun; dipping to pity
pilgrims held to the cracked earth
I lose altitude too fast
and reach for you to right myself:

> soaring laughing in the vast
> shining and ever edgeless space
> do you feel my wing tip brushing yours?

## I Am Tormented by Beauty

I am tormented by beauty
it will not leave me alone
just when I think I am safe
it sneaks around
in the fog-filtered morning
assaults me with unbearable songs
stabs to the heart
from my child's eyes
dissolves me
through a beacon face

When I might have wished
for limbo,
throat and lips
crave this presence swallowing me—-
heaven a breath removed
from such sweet hell

## Hope

*(after Emily Dickinson)*

Seeing my shutters open wide
attracted by the laughter
this forward fledgling swoops inside
to perch beneath my rafters

from where it chirps incessantly
"Perhaps ... some day" and "Why not?"
and "Stranger things have come to be"
I scoff "You're cracked" and try not

to listen to the chattering crake
that mocks at intellect —
fling it a crumb for pity's sake
or wring its ridiculous neck.

We meet in a crowd
with a brief and easy embrace
and possibilities shimmer between us

Left by ourselves
we inhabit a formal space
the shimmer consigned to a careful distance

### Because I Am Maimed

Because I am maimed
you look on me tenderly,
in a sense
seeing me as a child;
especially when
you've had something to drink
sentiment undoes your face;
onlookers could think
there is something between us—
few would see
it is an absence.

## Out on a Limb

Sliding out of the bath
bare body illusively lithe
oblivious of mechanisms
I find myself upright
and almost amazed
in this season of late blooming
that I haven't grown a new limb
casually as a silver maple
sending out another shoot

Stepping into the sun
I walk to music
that possibly only I can hear
bearing me on its quickening beat
until it seems I will have to run
feet skimming the ground
negating the weight
of wood and plastic and steel

Cruising lanes and highways
at the legal limits of speed
through bleak or dazzling landscape
I dance behind the wheel
to Disco, Dixieland, Vivaldi
all of it one
with gut and muscle and bone

When they find my body
resting in a ditch
prosthesis dangling Dali-like
from a cherry tree
tell them at the inquest
'she went happy'

## Skating Among the Graves

I pass a cemetery
on my way to work
and see perhaps myself
skating among the graves
impossibly fleet
one foot in the air
shouting "Hello down there
thanks for the lovely rink"

I am thinking of leaving
my body to Science
if I can watch
as they sliver my brain
decipher my innards
and disentangle the knots

*So that was the cause*
*of her Rues and Awes ...*
*Here is the root*
*of the Hems and Haws ...*
*Well I' ll be damned*
*a silver shiver*
*this side of sanity*

When I was I
I danced a spree
took off my clothes
and threw them away
freeing my flesh
to featherings of the air

In this mirror or that
the Wrath of God
or Universal Vamp
at this angle or that
adorable golden globes
or pitiful sacs
nonetheless breasts
lamented at twenty
now tenderly owned

The bridegroom values
willing clay
over alabaster
closing his eyes
to know the more
not see the less
if he were here
but only the bloodless air
fingers my friendless skin

beyond caresses
swooping and whooping
among the graves
flawlessly fleet
both feet in the air
calling "Hello
Hello out there
come skate on my lovely rink"

The Science Centre
Chief of Staff
not knowing the half
of it blinks
*Amazing ... simply amazing*

### *In the Prosthetics Fitting Room*

Stranded here all day
for adjustments
to an ill-fitting limb,
writing a poem about you
who are so much more
a part of me.

## *Birthday Song*

Waiting warm in the ageless dark
these wise little breasts
would leap to overflow
the heyday cupping of your hands

In the merry conspiracy of the dark
who would think to measure
this poverty of limbs
confused with your blessed complement

Singing from every aging inch
atoned in the elegant dark
these bones would suit you well
free of blinding facts of light

### *How Do I Know He Loves Me?*

How do I know he loves me? By the way
He never gazes deeply in my eyes
Or has a sentimental word to say
Or stops me in my tracks with Whats and Whys
And never quips of my advancing years
Or devastates me with indifferent touch
Or sends me into storms of bitter tears
Or chills me with Now hold it, that's too much;
This is not proof he loves me I admit
Or ever dreams of dreaming on my breast
But my slender case concerns me not a bit
He only shines, the devil take the rest:
Unabashed, I hold as Pentecost
The fact he hasn't told me to get lost.

## Dearest, I Will Not

Dearest, I will not fly away with you
To rollicking continents or spangled seas
Or settle in a cottage with a view
Or loose a fierce inferno though I freeze;
I will not steal a golden afternoon
To make some little room a Paradise
Or hold you at the mercy of the moon
Or pilfer stars though darkness be the price;
I will not undermine taught modesties
By throwing furtive crumbs to wry desire
Or take a berth on chartless odysseys
But stay and tend a hearth that balks at fire:
Fair and square, I buckle to my task
But who knows what I'd do if you should ask.

Tender secrets
meaning to unfold
to you at the perfect mutual season

burst in blossomings
reason cannot hold
petals flinging out of context

### *Out of the Darkness*

If you are going to
think about the city
you have to think about light,
the one essential
scene setter.

The pitiless August sun
with no such nonsense
as dulling sharp edges
or softening corners,
lights the city of steel
and concrete and glass
and plazas and parking lots,
the meadowless
vistaless
stiff-visaged town,
exposing its sins
like a just-before-drowning
revelation of conscience.

A tantalizing glimmer
touches the muffled
gray-swathed city,
slides around
the edge of its shroud
making tentative darts
and teasing promises,
then sneaks away
leaving no glint
in the smothering gloom.

The icy light
of star-dancing moon-nights
striking crystal fires
from frivolous snowflakes
before they merge
in anonymous slush.

Tongues of fire
on five-cent candles
anxiously wedged
between warped claws
of iron luminaries
as the pious drop their coins
and say their ancient prayers.

Christmas light
strings itself out
from door to eave
to roof antenna,
tangles in twigs
weaves through evergreens
times its twinkles
forgets
to turn itself off
when windows go blind.

Neons, beautiful
seen through tears
or blurred
on rain-sloshed pavements
or perceived by astigmatics
without their glasses.

The almost light
of crowded bars,
the mind-blinding lights
at teenage dances,
the gap-toothed lights
of the government building
the misted rainbow
lights of a fountain.

Single scattered lights
dropped but not drowned
in the harbour's liquid glass
and strewn like beads
from a broken necklace
in the creases and folds
of the corrugated town.

Miles away
whispering down
the paradoxical silver thaw
with jewels encases
the twig
the bough
the cable
the pole
(built to withstand
three times the typical load)
till brilliantly sparkling
it breaks something's back

and the lights of the city go out.

### Out of the Corner of the Eye

Out of the corner of the eye
glimpses of grotesqueries
or dancing movements
slight as butterflies

Almost beyond the range of hearing
elusive sounds
of hopeless sirens
or golden notes on a gypsy breeze

The head almost jerks
with a vertigo gone before it came
and the breast momentarily jolts
with heart's tumult or breath-stop

We search among our potions
for a panacea
to flesh the phantoms of joy
and forestall the incipient pain

## Lullaby One

Some stop short
of bearing innocence;
like finely bubbled glass
it cries for cherishing,
the touch that it invites
is velvet gentle
steadier than love,
the brusque or falter-fingered grasp
may shatter it
a breath blemish.

Redolent of moonstone
itself the only reason for its glow
it quickens hope
among the optimists
while others read reproach
in its unblinking gaze
or forecast early doom
for such serenity.

Moonstone
millstone
ache or anodyne
we fill a space
with flesh made word
and crown ourselves
with halos, thorns.

### Facades

I passed a house today
with trees held up before its face
as if ashamed
alone behind a millioned mask
of contradictory leaves
like a soul enfoliaged by frivolity
or hedged with brittle twigs
of spite or caustic wit

Ironic gusts will devastate the blind
disclosing sanctuary, derelict, or ruin

Look-twice blossoms
haphazard in the grass
factory red, yellow, blue

Will the children return
after I have passed
to look for their abandoned toys?

### *Eight-Year-Old*

You say you'd like to stay a child
because as you grow up
you'll have to learn
to work
to drive
to buy
to be a boyfriend
husband
father

And then you say
a child doesn't have it easy
there are monsters
in your sleep
and you wish you had more friends
you talk to everyone
getting laughs at your joking
but they do not come to play
and Brian doesn't like you

Don't cry
don't try so hard
he will
you will grow up

After the bath
spotless and serene
my alabaster angel-child

Before the bath
fight-to-the-finish scene
grimy little alabastard

## *October Icons*

God or Angel of whitest light
gliding across my four-in-the-morning sky
flooding the corners of my space
near-blinding me to certainties of noon

manuscripts of whitest light
opening slowly along a shelf of air
the turning leaves inviting me
to read aloud new secrets of myself

dark-shining eye-dance
has blazed these icons on my October sky
melting commonplace conceptions
of must-be night or day, black or white

though the figure of light fall to earth
and skyheld scripts admit of no translation
this light will gleam in dreamless mornings
lancing clear of lost-to-me dark eyes

### Why Should I Analyze

Why should I analyze
rib-tightening and gut-alert
that grip me
at the thought of you
or the sound of your voice,
when three notes on a clarinet
or midnight moon-spill
on the kitchen floor
can startle me into
primitive percussions

## Wish for a Wind

I sewed a clown
a cuddly toy
and made the head too big
but let it be
for the head is more
than legs and body and arms

I look at you
and I look at me
two level heads
two bright balloons
on tight-held strings

I wish for a wind
to snatch the strings
free the bright balloons
and float them away
leaving our simple selves
to our simple pleasures

I
begin by
making a chain
of the required length
in a neutral shade and build on
it in taut half-double crochet to make
myself a mat but I dream of you and free-form
a     wider     mesh     in     carnival
colors     and     the     question
is     will     I     revert     to     the
pattern and complete
my chosen piece
of work or
turn it
into
a
kite
that
you
and
I

c
a
n

m
e
r
r
i
l
y
g
o
a
n
d
f
l
y

### A Sort of Te Deum

There's something to be said
for neon signs and radios,
driving on rainy nights
and having to go all alone;
the sp lled out reds and greens
of galvanized inanities
lie in soft abstraction
along the sloshed pavement
while dialled violins
annihilate commentators
to follow twin batons
that flick aside capricious rain
and I an urban Eve
in six-cylindered solitude
praise the unwitting gods
of accidental ecstasies.

A face, a reed,
a phrase, a fugue heart-freeing —
once-comforts now are exultations;

amazed at
this bounty of well-being
I wonder what axe is waiting to fall.

...

A smile, a leaf,
a word, a note soul-spearing —
exultation swells to heartburst;

circled in light
though the source of it elsewhering
let every axe in creation fall.

45

## Amputation

Father Phonsus makes his rounds
and says he's glad to see me still alive,
some other patient with my name
has done with troubling to survive
and so I offer thanks
that I was not the one
released from betraying flesh
disintegrating bone
for flesh and bone bedevil hope
but hope will still contrive.

Each of us has found a way
to immunize against the penalties
that bed us here in sisterhood;
one marks time with pale profanities
while some roll bandages
or bait cantankerousness
or find escape within a book
where life is neatly bound,
Thy-will-be-doners count their prayers
for prayers sometimes appease.

One ... two ... three ... four ...
Sodium Pentothal seeps into a vein,
the count fades, and swaying circles
dip and rise in orbit round my brain
and then I'm floating up
and chanting drunkenly
Doctor Duncan is a doll ...
a doll ... a doll ... a god ...
God the Doctor, Doctor God
and God has need of pain.

At last I leave the regions where
old omens of oblivion revolve,
unreasoned hope is justified
for Doctor God has chosen to absolve
the smirched anatomy;
with mercy-sharpened blade
excised the gangrenous offence
and washed his hands of it
leaving a blank and blameless space
a space for me to solve.

## Fitness, Fun, and Fellowship

### 1

In the Adapted Aquatics Class
at Wedgwood Park on Saturday,
modesty prevails.
We are all quick-change artists
clever with towels and twists and turns
screening ourselves from one another:
trim little girl, hefty mother,
a Venus or two,
I more shy for my scrawny chest
than for my leg
that ends at the knee,
the only ones honestly unselfconscious
the young women
supposed to be retarded.

In the pool
we are more ourselves.
The girl with spastic limbs
and futile tongue
finds the water friendlier than air;
it flows to her flailings,
laps at her flawless breasts and thighs
that ache to be caressed
by our gentle-handed coach,
his compassion so palpable
I too might mistake it for lust.

In my element
blessedly buoyant
I float and swim
not far
but free of all contrivances,
at the price of chlorine-tortured
eyes, nose, and throat,
and anxious travel
with one foot and crutches
on wet, treacherous floors.

On a Tuesday at the Aquarena,
long-legged girls with solarium skin
and black pub(l)ic hair
saunter through
their post-swim performance
of shampoo, shower, blow-dry
and tossing of tresses,
paying no perceptible mind
to this paint-by-number portrait
waiting for a brush,
this candidate for miracles.

Prosthesis off
and swimsuit on
I stand with my crutches,
adjusting a loose screw
which nonetheless lets me down
to whack my knobby hip
on the stone cold floor.
The gorgeous goddesses
hardly notice.

I gave up swimming
and took to walking in the Park.

## 2

On a post-fifty birthday
with nothing exciting in view
but still in tune for Te Deums
I rushed to get ready for Mass
and stepped on a rug
I should have thrown away
before it tossed me to the floor
and broke my wrist—
though luckily not the one
needed to lean on my cane.

Compensation for the fall—
a walk in the Park
with my inscrutable friend,
his compassion so matter-of-fact
I might mistake it
for indifference.
Someone took our photograph
and I can see us now—
him at my left side,
me with my arm in a sling,
both of us grinning
and looking straight ahead,
close enough to touch,
but not.

# 3

A warm October eve
I park alone
at the edge of Mundy Pond,
lulled by water's small talk
in sight of St. Teresa's Church
and the Harry Mews Centre—
where I am on the waiting list
for Fitness, Fun, and Fellowship.
A snipe I know
wings in at my wish,
forages with quick bill
in the mud among the rushes,
lights on a rock and nods to me
  *Yes*
  *Yes*
  *Yes*
across reflections.

Winter is on the way
and what will a cripple do then,
poor thing?

Hide from the storm
and keep herself warm,
or go out in the wind
for a fling, fling, fling,
go out in the wind for a fling.

### Why I Never Went to Lourdes

My phantom foot is stepping out
My deafened ear is ringing
My meagre bosom swells with love
My quinsy throat is singing

My underactive thyroid gland
sends energizing surges
and gustier than in girlhood days
rise elemental urges

Neurotic notions laugh to death
and my astigmatic vision
transforms the merely beautiful
with exquisite precision

The heart can only hold so much
of joy within its border —
I fear I'd flip if all my parts
were present and in order

I am translating
statements of sweet clover
in front of St. Teresa's Church,

forget-me-nots
where the Premier gazes over
and bachelor buttons at the University.

## Two Places

I have no deep desire
to go to Rome or Spain
but nearer home
two places haunt me
intermittently:
remote Grand Bruit
(they say on the coast Grand Britt)
and volatile St. Pierre.

The only apparent happening
in Grand Bruit
is the waterfall;
I don't remember the people there,
only unexpected sheep
grazing beside the steepled church,
the outer reaches being
a small rocky beach
and not ten minutes west
a lily pond
with always, from Centre Stage,
the sound of crashing water
the Grand Bruit.

St. Pierre, on the other hand,
is a happening:
pilgrims climb chanting
to a hillside shrine
while tourists treasure hunt
for booze, Chanel,
and pure wool turtlenecks;
I am tipsy from sipping
Cuarenta y Tres
and fancied by a wedding guest
dancing at Savoyard;
the sound of stuck pigs
reaches up the road
to the eerie graveyard,
the organist weeps in his beer
for the stuck pigs
while kites lunge free
toward Langlade and Miquelon.

Grand Bruit
haunts my waking
and St. Pierre my sleep.

## Sparable for Sandra

Mid moss-moaning
and riotous poppy-shouting,
the delicate statement of the rose

shows no sign
of the mistake in doubting
the durable stem, the quick thorn

The torch slips
the twirler grips the flame
her fingers do not feel the heat

Even so
does the fire spare my frame
at your hand's help in this perilous place

### Sword of Damocles

I fear to use
this crystal dish
torn between
the joy of its beauty
and the dread
of breaking it

I could smash it now
and have the anguish
over with
or hide it on a shelf
depriving myself of joy
deferring loss

And what of persons
precious in my life

## I *Know What* I *Know*

*I* know what *I* know
*You* know what *you* know
no air of conspiracy
of a rOund shining secret
bOuncing between us

Our smiles are open
no innuendO
of the secret shining
of one or the other
eclipsing all others

*You* know what *you* know
*I* know what *I* know

## Summer Song

(May be sung to the air of Schubert's *Die Forelle*,
repeating the first and third stanzas)

You give me wild strawberries
tangy and sweet
fresh from the hillside
our eyes do not meet

You bring musky roses
white whispers of heat
in careful arrangement
our eyes do not meet

We walk by the ocean
stones trip my feet
your right hand upholds me
our eyes do not meet

What keeps me from kisses
tangy and sweet
What keeps me from kisses
our eyes do not meet
What keeps me from kisses
our eyes do not meet

### Twice in These Six Years

Twice in these six years our lips have met
So delicately I cannot recall
The shape or texture of your mouth at all
But precipice of warmth and stop of breath
The only kiss that I will not forget
A gift from you in the crowded Christmas hall
I should have thought your festal spirit all
That started up New Year conjecture yet
The Heart Upon My Sleeve a little torn
Today I kissed you on a chaffing word
And felt your breath suspended like a bird
Surprised in song or waiting to be born
Let's count to three then kiss for all we're worth
And in the process perish or give birth

## Starving

Starving
I try to make do
with the sparse rations
on my plate
but they refuse to be eaten;
I am allowed only a nibble or two
once in a blue moon,
anything extra triggers heartburn
makes me vow to fast.

Heart that I crave,
what do you take for sustenance?
Do you feast on secret stores
or dine light as a sparrow?
If you are hungry
gulp me down
and help yourself to more —
it may be too late
when the dinner bell sounds.

We          Isn't
are         it
a           time
pair        to
of          get
knitting   down
needles    to
you       business
plain     and
and       knit
I            this
purl        mountain
into       of
sample    yarn
swatches  into
of          a
new       rainbow
hues      to
and       wrap
complex  ourselves
textures  in

Two starlings on a high wire

dally at a ritual distance

smug in the platinum sun

## *A Gull on the Parking Lot*

Squat feathered
dawdler on the pavement
self-exile
inches from my wheels
how pedestrian
what a fall
from grace

## A Peacock Is a Paper Clip

"A peacock is a paper clip" my mentor said
"and not-yet-fledgling writers
may as well get it into their heads
that when begging assignments
no more serious topic is likely to be set
for of giving assignments
I have a most unprofessorlike dread".

Was it playfulness, perverseness, or caprice
or merely an effort to grant surcease
to mesmerising thoughts
of Violets, Moonlight, and Autumn Leaves?
Suddenly aware of the paper clip turning between his  fingers
he may have sought for something
most unlike to pair with it.
What more unlikely than a peacock,
than which nothing could be more vain
in a world held together by mechanical contrivances.

The only well-known fact about the bird is that
when spreading its tail it displays some beautiful feathers—
a pleasant thought
I would have been glad to preserve intact
were it not for a disillusioning statement
by St. Francis de Sales
who says that when spreading their brilliant feathers
they ruffle the rest and make themselves ugly.
(He also says that rabbits are white in winter
because of eating snow.)
I know the Saint was not at his best
when explaining natural wonders
but his having anticipated by three and a half centuries
all my spiritual blunders
makes me inclined
to keep even his most whimsical notions in mind.

I doubt that even St. Francis would suggest
having peacocks around the office
with papers in their beaks —
another answer I must seek,
not wishing to prove my mentor wrong.

After lessons from an Eskimo
skilled in cat's cradling figures
out of limp, monotonous string
I shall bend our plain, utilitarian metal loops
into long-horned steers, peacocks, lumberjacks,
beauty contest winners, and chicken coops.
What more subtle way to impress
the enthusiastic hypochondriac, musician, birdwatcher,
or otherwise oddly inclined fellow
than by securing his papers with a clean-lined physician,
tempered steel clavichord, or yellow-bellied sapsucker.
The peacock clip should be reserved for those
whose few good qualities are overshadowed
by their pose of self-importance.

Someone (as yet uncanonized though paraphrased) has said
"Make a better paper clip
and the world will beat a path to your door".
For my inevitable fame, let me now bless
the unprofessorial head of my aforementioned mentor.

### At a Poetry Reading on Holy Thursday

Trapped by obligingness
and scarcely acknowledged
yen for fame
I stand here in my long dress
and borrowed mane
trying to make the scene
when I should be
on my knees in church.

This poem started
during Palm Sunday Mass
to the twanging of guitars
*Come let's share*
*in the supper of the Lord*
*in the Blessed Sacrament*
while in my brain
there quavered plaintively
*tantum ergo Sacramentum*
*veneremur cernui.*

Old forms
surely have departed
do newer rites of grace prevail?
In any case
I still would justify
my apparent failure
to give equal time
to penance and good works
and my having absented myself
this solemn evening
from the parish church.

Is it not penance
exposing a tame talent
in proximity
with stuff of wilder substance?
and yet there may be
a word, a nuance,
a trick of sound
whose merit will tinkle
if not resound
to the greater glory of God
and be a gift to you
temples of his Spirit.

Share my crumbs!
Every poem
is a sort of Alleluia.

## *Caprice*

There they hang, neatly framed, in Pitts Memorial Hall
The Executive Committee of the Methodist College
Board of Governors 1895 – '96
Sitting and standing, eyes front, most properly attired
Complete with spats, bowler hats, and walking sticks
There they have hung, for all I know, undisturbed
In black and white since 1895 – '96.

The other day, nationally famous, the Ballet came onstage
The placement of lights and the staging conspired
To produce one of art's most whimsical tricks
Leaping and gliding lithe limbs in tights
        and warm-hued tutus
Danced inside the frame over eyes transfixed
The neatly framed Methodists I think enjoyed it
But their absent wives of 1895 – '96?

### Beached

Try this
young poet
middle poet
elder poet

Leave yourself out of it

Say you are writing
about a beach
Who wants to hear
how you relate to the beach
or if you found something
especially yourself
among the rocks

What we want
is the beach's side of the story

A beach may write a poem
on itself
but it won't be published
unless you copy it down

# *He Went Gentle*

He went 'gentle into that good night'
and I would not wish it otherwise
for gentle he doubtless came
from that other night
his mother being oh so gentle
or, more precise, unruffleable,
and more or less gentle flowed his life.

Not all went well, far from it,
but the 'slings and arrows' evoked from him
no more than a shrug and a wry smile,
and though some would suggest
he forged the slings and arrows himself
who knows that it could have been
any other way.

Humor he had plenty of, though not
the rambunctious kind;
rather the kind that said to one
who smashed a glass on the kitchen floor
"Why wait till you had it washed and dried?"
That was it, really, in a nutshell;
it was always the irony he saw, never the tragedy.
Is there any tragedy after all
but the tragedy of no sense of humor?

A dreamer he was too
who studied money-making formulas
and went so far as concocting one
peddling it round with a pony
that he couldn't afford to keep,
long after it ceased to be commercially sound
for any entrepreneur
to home-mix javel water.

Teller of tales, singer of songs,
player of games with his children,
sporadic winner of bread,
irascible taker of dole,
unbossable jack of all trades
blessed with a good and practical wife
who finally took in boarders.

Father at last of a long awaited boy
who in much less time
than he had been eagerly longed for
departed to the place from where
(as he answered himself
when wondering how someone got to Heaven)
"God let down a rope and pulled him up."

He didn't talk about things like that
and he didn't talk about God either
or not very much
(Church was the kitchen on Sunday
with the radio playing *Lead Kindly Light*)
I can only remember once or twice:
once, and this was near the end,
when the pastor invited him to pray,
"I didn't bother Him much in my life
and I won't go tormenting him now."
And again, on hearing the news of the world,
"The trouble is they don't believe in God."

Fond of the drink himself
he saw the humor, the fittingness
of habitual drunks
and feeble old men with eerie rituals;
he extracted and savored
the incorrigible glee
from 'hopelessly wasted lives'.
To many he was one of them
"never amounted to anything

but a nice fellow all the same
with a dry sense of humor"
they were sorry to see him go
relatively young, of a chronic disease
that had never been quite believed
by anyone but himself till it was nearly over.

There was something I wanted not to believe
but of course it had to be true.
I don't remember the words he used
and I heard it only once
but the gist of it was this
"I won't last much longer
and the sooner I'm dead the better."
And who could argue it,
for if any dreams were left
pain would have washed the last away,
there was nothing that he had to do
but wait.

And when the time came
"I'd like a drink" he said,
for once meaning water only
and too far launched in that good night
to make a final quip
he turned his head and breathed
"Ah, that feels good."
A daughter cried
"Is it Heaven he's gone to, or Hell?"
But she knew after just a little reflection
that his not unspotted soul
might have to go on a waiting list
but must eventually get in.

## I Wait to Be Overwhelmed With Grief

I wait to be overwhelmed with grief
not simply cleansed
in the sweet emotion
aroused by *Amazing Grace*
but shaken pitilessly with panic
at irrevocable loss

For more than forty years
she mothered me
not hovering
but cautiously concerned
almost with diffidence
because I was the first-born
because I was different

Afraid perhaps
to see into the depths
there was no prying
into private griefs
but we were always present
to each other

And now when I reach for the phone
and remember she is not there
maybe I should welcome
a wild outpouring
for I wonder how insidiously
what lies too deep for tears
may take its toll

### The Way of the Cross

The organ was stilled
and statues hid in purple cloth,
with a sense of satisfying desolation
we attended Mass
and went around the Stations.

We gave up candy,
meat, and random snacks
refrained from dances
said extra Rosaries
and shunned immodest glances.

We attended the scarifying Missions
drowsed in incense
roused to sing our Stabat Maters
confessed our sins and received the Eucharist —
the Church's faithful sons and daughters.

Old modes of penance
have been cast aside
we eat and drink, make merry any day
midst terrors of the body, soul, and mind
to live with equanimity is to pray.

### On My Death by Drowning

Especially the ones who knew me well
Will think this final trysting with the sea
A tragic chance for I could never be
Disconsolate even at the edge of hell
And so at last when I was free to tell
That you and I had opened into we
The banquet spread with every delicacy
Why would I change eureka to farewell
You alone if anyone may gauge
How wise I was to keep my grateful scheme
To close the story on this perfect page
And leave you at the apex of the dream —
So speaks the romantic but I choose old age
And the risk of salmonella in the cream.

### Autumn Song

when all the world was green and blue
and you were young and clever
you wisely waited for the who
would be your all forever

the dandelion went to seed
the sun kept on blaspheming
bereft you fed the lesser need
said you had been dreaming

then after all who blazed in sight
so young and wise and clever
and now you lie here in the night
more alone than ever

### The Time Will Come

the time will come to repossess
the rooms we occupied
to taste again the bread and wine
this interim denied

and by the fire once again
we'll tell each other how
we learned to turn the calendar
till sometime should be now

and we will soar beyond the reach
we early learned to fly
and wake together after rain
to a white remembered sky

for once at last and evermore
resplendent past the sun
we'll do again the selfsame things
that we have never done

I'd like to feel the quicksilver length of you
indented along the inquisitive length of me
   … just briefly
       … that's all
         … I think

### *I Will Not Go So Far*

I will not go so far as to say
that all these songs and snippets
visited on you
have been so much folderol
I meant it all

I will not go so far as to say
I should have skipped the frills
and got to the point
the truth is I enjoyed it
like hiding coins
in a steaming bowl of colcannon

But enough is enough
my next poem will be one word
maybe not even that

Sparrow fluttering
on my shut-in tree
have you left the sky to visit

or full-fledged
sprung into Nativity
from last year's paper decoration

## *Purple Iris*

Purple iris in a bog
to the blue edge of my vision;
snowy geese in cool precision
gliding silent; veils of fog
trailing over morning meadows;
green niagaras of the sea
thundering down to pleasure me;
rainbow echoes; river shadows;
tapestry of talk and laughter;
bashful and risqué duet
of aspen leaf and clarinet;
forgetfulness of then and after:
miscellany to see me through
times I cannot be with you.

### *After Reading Thoreau's* Walden

Lead me to a small
but well-appointed cell
free of accoutrements
that flusterate the mind
serve me with celerity
when I ring the bell
but don't leave any
bric-a-brac behind

Take away the rondo
once it's played
take away the novel
once it's read
leave no clutter
in my cell
leave no clutter
in my head

Bring me
a single visitor
only now and then
but let me keep
a dictionary
paper
and a pen

## A Note on the Text

Some of the poems in this book have appeared in the following: *From This Place; Pottersfield Portfolio; Newfoundland Quarterly; Landings; Canadian Poetry; TickleAce; Scruncheons; East of Canada; Canadian Literature; CVII; A Woman's Almanac; 31 Newfoundland Poets; Mamashee; Riverine; Alberta Poetry Yearbook; Banked Fires; Easterly; Newfoundland Writers 1974; A Poem In My Soup; Writers of Newfoundland and Labrador; A Way with Words; The Evening Telegram;* and *Robinson-Blackmore* newspapers and periodicals. Some of the poems have been included in dramatic presentations at the Basement Theatre, St. John's. *A Peacock is a Paper Clip, At a Poetry Reading on Holy Thursday, He Went Gentle,* and *Sword of Damocles* were awarded prizes in the Newfoundland Arts and Letters Competition.

The sparable as a poetic form is the invention of the author, beginning serendipitously with *After the Bath.* The original sparable (variation of sparrow bill) was a small, sharp headless tack used by shoemakers.

The author wishes to thank Carmelita McGrath for her fine editing; members of the Newfoundland Writers' Guild and the Writers' Alliance of Newfoundland and Labrador; and the Newfoundland and Labrador Arts Council. Very special thanks to Bernice Morgan and Helen Porter.

# Alphabetical Index